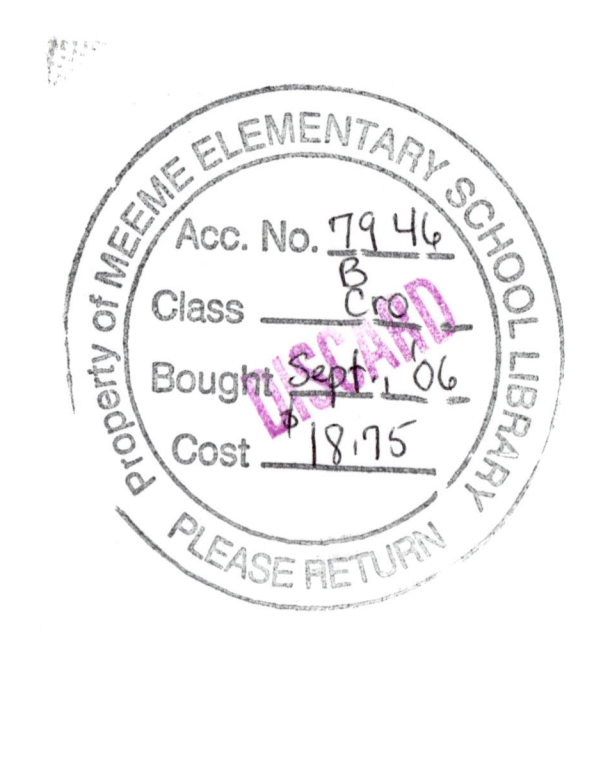

American Lives

Davy Crockett

Rick Burke

Heinemann Library
Chicago, Illinois

© 2004 Heinemann Library
a division of Reed Elsevier Inc.
Chicago, Illinois

Customer Service 888-454-2279
Visit our website at www.heinemannlibrary.com

All rights reserved. No part of this publication may be reproduced or transmitted in any form or by any means, electronic or mechanical, including photocopying, recording, taping, or any information storage and retrieval system, without permission in writing from the publisher.

Designed by Sarah Figlio
Photo research by Kathy Creech
Printed and Bound in the United States by Lake Book Manufacturing, Inc.

08 07 06 05 04
10 9 8 7 6 5 4 3 2 1

Library of Congress Cataloging-in-Publication Data
Burke, Rick, 1957-
  Davy Crockett / by Rick Burke.
    v. cm. -- (American lives)
Includes bibliographical references (p.) and index.
Contents: Fight! -- Family -- Driving the herd -- Runaway -- Alone --Polly -- War -- New wife -- Helping Tennessee -- Congress --Disappointment -- Remember the Alamo --Remembering Davy.
  ISBN 1-4034-4190-1 -- ISBN 1-4034-4198-7 (pbk.)
1. Crockett, Davy, 1786-1836--Juvenile literature. 2. Pioneers--Tennessee--Biography--Juvenile literature. 3. Frontier and pioneer life--Tennessee--Juvenile literature. 4. Tennessee--Biography--Juvenile literature. 5. Legislators--United States--Biography--Juvenile literature. 6. United States. Congress. House--Biography--Juvenile literature. 7. Alamo (San Antonio, Tex.)--Siege, 1836--Juvenile literature.
[1. Crockett, Davy, 1786-1836. 2. Pioneers. 3. Legislators.] I. Title. II. American lives (Heinemann Library (Firm))
F436.C95B875 2003
  976.8'04'092--dc21

2003004974

Acknowledgments
The author and publishers are grateful to the following for permission to reproduce copyright material: Title page, p. 4 Burstein Collection/Corbis; pp. 5, 11, 27, 29 Texas State Library and Archives Commission; p. 6 Michael Maslan Historic Photographs/Corbis; p. 7 Hulton-Deutsch Collection/Corbis; p. 8 The Crockett Tavern Museum; pp. 9, 16, 26 Hulton Archive/Getty Images; p. 10 Francis G. Mayer/Corbis; p. 12 The Mariner's Museum/Corbis; pp. 13, 21 Corbis; p. 14 Museum of the City of New York/Corbis; pp. 15, 20, 22, 28 Bettmann/Corbis; pp. 17, 24 The Granger Collection, New York; p. 18 Joslyn Art Museum, Omaha, Nebraska; p. 19 N. Carter/North Wind Picture Archives; p. 23 Archivo Iconografico, S. A./Corbis; p. 25 Stock Montage, Inc.

Cover photograph by Bettmann/Corbis

The publisher would like to thank Michelle Rimsa for her comments in the preparation of this book.

Every effort has been made to contact copyright holders of any material reproduced in this book. Any omissions will be rectified in subsequent printings if notice is given to the publisher.

Some words are shown in bold, **like this.** You can find out what they mean by looking in the glossary.

For more information on the image of Davy Crockett that appears on the cover of this book, turn to page 4.

Contents

Fight! 4
Family 6
Driving the Herd 8
Runaway 10
Alone 12
Polly 14
War 16
New Wife .18
Helping Tennessee 20
Congress .22
Disappointment 24
Remember the Alamo! 26
Remembering Davy 28
Glossary 30
More Books to Read 31
Places to Visit 31
Index 32

Fight!

Davy Crockett looked over the wall of the **fort**, in San Antonio, Texas, and saw his enemy. Hundreds of Mexican soldiers stood together outside, waiting for the order from their general to attack. Davy and the 182 other men inside the Alamo knew there was little chance of walking away from the battle alive. Davy and the others were fighting for the freedom of Texas. It was March 1836, and the land of Texas was part of the country of Mexico.

Davy Crockett became one of the most famous **frontiersmen** of the United States.

On the morning of March 6, 1836, General Santa Anna, shown here on a white horse, recaptured the Alamo for Mexico.

The Mexican army of General Antonio López de Santa Anna had attacked the fort for thirteen days in a row. Santa Anna wanted the Texans to **surrender,** but they refused. The **commander** of the Alamo, Colonel William Travis, knew that protecting the Alamo was very important in the plan to free Texas. When the Mexican army came over the walls of the Alamo, Davy Crockett, Colonel Travis, and the men with them fought with all their strength. Though they lost the fight, they made history as heroes.

Family

David Crockett was born on August 17, 1786, in Greene County, Tennessee. Davy's parents were John and Rebecca Crockett. Davy had five brothers and three sisters. John tried hard to be a good businessman, but he never had much luck earning money for his family.

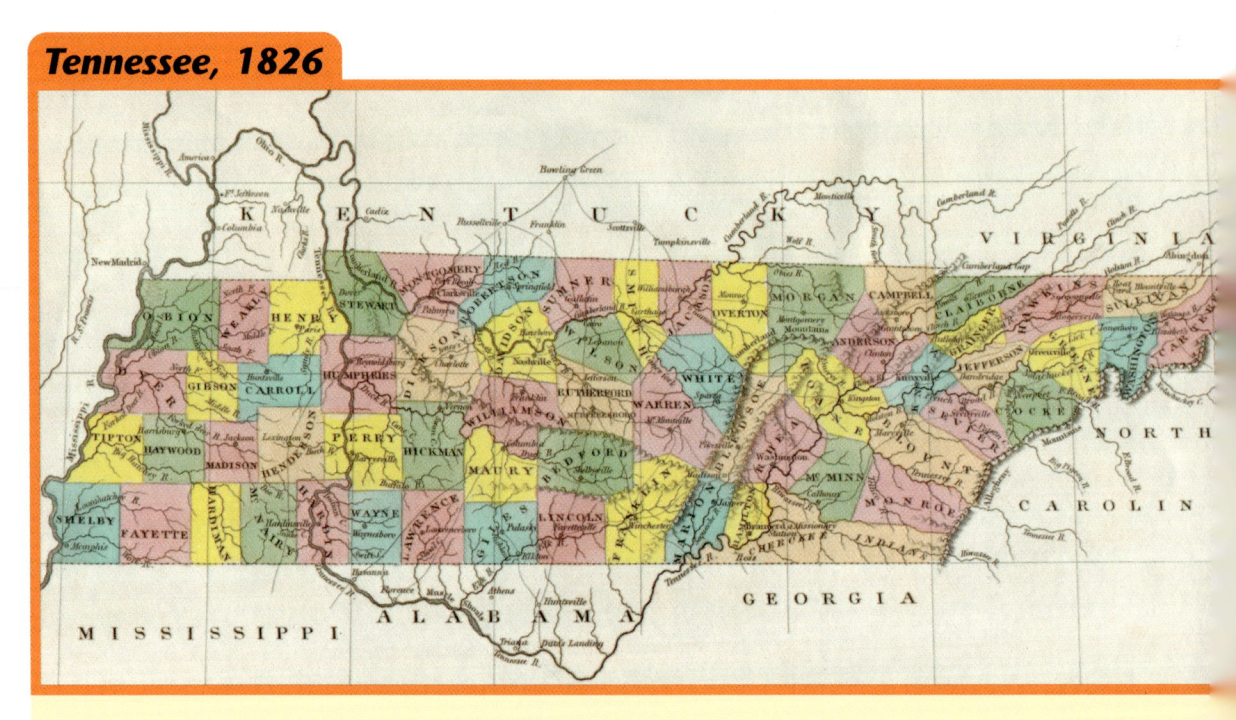

Tennessee, 1826

Davy Crockett lived in Tennessee for many years. Today, there is a town named Crockett, Tennessee.

The Life of Davy Crockett

1786	1799	1802	1806
Born on August 17, in Greene County, Tennessee	Ran away from home	Returned home	Married Mary Finley (Polly)

Farmers brought wagons full of grain to mills to be ground. Davy's father owned a flour mill.

Davy's father had bad luck with jobs. When Davy was a small boy, John opened a flour **mill.** Soon after, the river flooded and washed away the mill. John was not very good at farming either, so he bought a **tavern.** In his father's tavern, Davy learned how to tell stories that made people laugh. Davy used this skill for the rest of his life.

1813	**1815**	**1821**	**1836**
Fought in the Creek War	*Married Elizabeth Patton*	*Elected to the Tennessee* **legislature**	*Fought in the Battle of the Alamo. Died March 6*

Driving the Herd

Davy loved to be outside. When he was a young boy, he learned how to hunt. He became very good at it. Davy's family was poor, so he hunted animals for food for his family. Davy soon got a chance to help his family by earning money in another way, as well.

Telling Tales

One of Davy's stories was that he killed a bear with just a knife when he was three years old. Another story said that Davy could shoot out the flame of a candle with his rifle from 300 feet (91 meters) away.

Davy's father opened this tavern in 1796. Davy spent evenings there, listening to traveler's stories.

Once Davy arrived in Virginia with the cows, he stayed for a few weeks to help take care of them. All cows had to be milked several times a day.

When Davy was twelve years old, a traveler at the **tavern** gave Davy a job. The man paid Davy six dollars to help him move his herd of cows from Tennessee to a farm in Virginia. Davy was young to be away from home, but his family needed the money. Davy took the job and did well. The farmer wanted Davy to stay in Virginia, but he missed his family and returned to Tennessee to be with them.

Runaway

When Davy was thirteen, his father sent him to school to learn to read and write. At the school was a boy who liked to tease and beat up the younger children. Davy thought the boy needed to be taught not to treat other people that way. After school one day, Davy waited in the bushes for the bully to come by. Davy jumped out and attacked the boy. Davy scratched the boy's face and made him cry.

When Davy was young, children of all ages were taught in one schoolroom by a teacher.

A children's song says that Davy "killed him a bear when he was only three." That idea was probably from one of Davy's stories. However, Davy was a skilled hunter as a boy.

Davy knew that when he went to school the next day, the teacher would punish him for fighting. Davy decided not to go back to school. He spent the day in the woods. The teacher wrote Davy's father a letter, asking why Davy was not in school. To keep from being punished by both the teacher and his father, Davy ran away from home. Davy walked to Virginia and spent the next three years working away from home.

Alone

At first, Davy worked on farms in Virginia. He worked hard and was able to save seven dollars, which was a lot of money when Davy was young. Davy traveled to Baltimore, Maryland. Baltimore was a city that ships sailed to from around the world because of its big **harbor.** When Davy saw the ships, his dream was to get a job on a ship and see different countries. Davy gave all his money to a friend to keep safe while Davy went to ask for a job on a ship.

Ships like these traveled all over the world, carrying people and goods.

Dinnertime at the tavern was busy. Many people came to eat and tell their stories of travelling.

Davy's friend stole the money. Davy's dream of being a sailor ended. Davy was sad, but the idea of going home to Tennessee made him feel better. Davy began the long journey back to his parents' **tavern** and arrived there around dinnertime. At first, his family thought he was just another tired traveler stopping for a meal. His sister finally realized who he really was. His family stopped what they were doing. They hurried over to him and spent the evening hugging, laughing, and listening to Davy's stories.

Polly

While Davy was away from home, his family had some troubles. Davy's father, John Crockett, borrowed money from his neighbors, and he was not able to pay it back. He owed a farmer named Abraham Wilson $36. Davy worked on Wilson's farm every day for six months until the **debt** was paid off. Davy then worked every day for another six months on John Kennedy's farm until his father's $40 debt to him was paid off, too.

Davy was a hard worker. This helped him be successful later in life when he was out on his own.

John Kennedy was a nice man, and he treated Davy well. After the debt was paid, Davy kept working on the Kennedy farm. Kennedy's son, who was a teacher, taught Davy how to read and write. When Davy was nineteen, he went to a dance at a nearby farm. While he was there, he saw a beautiful young girl named Mary Finley, who everyone called Polly. Davy fell in love with her. After a few months, he asked her to marry him. They were married on August 16, 1806.

People in Davy's time used schoolbooks like this one to learn how to read.

War

Davy and Polly rented a farm near the Finley family. Within a few years, they had two sons—John Wesley and William. Davy and Polly worked hard on their farm, but Davy was not very good at earning money. Davy thought he could make more money farming in a different part of Tennessee. In 1811, the Crockett family moved west to land near the Elk River.

Farming was hard work. Raising animals and growing food took care of the family's needs.

During the Creek War, Davy was a member of the Tennessee Volunteer Mounted Riflemen.

In 1812, the United States went to war with Britain. That year, Polly had her third child. Davy and Polly named her Margaret. The Crocketts then moved further west to Bean's Creek. In 1813, Davy joined other men of Tennessee to fight in the **militia** against the British. Davy also fought in several battles of the Creek War, against Creek warriors. The Native Americans were not fighting for the British. They were protecting their land.

The Ballad of Davy Crockett

A song titled "The Ballad of Davy Crockett" tells the story of what Davy did during the Creek War. The song was written in 1954 for a movie about Davy's life.

New Wife

In 1814, the war ended. Davy returned home. A few weeks later, Polly got sick and died. It was hard for Davy to raise three children all by himself. Davy met a woman named Elizabeth Patton who lived near Davy's farm. Elizabeth's husband had been killed in the Creek War. Davy married Elizabeth in the summer of 1815.

Many people married as a way to provide a good home for their children. Men brought home food while the women took care of the children and the home.

Mills and distilleries had to be built near rivers and streams. Running water provided the power needed to run the machinery.

Davy and Elizabeth, along with Davy's three children and Elizabeth's two children, moved to Shoal Creek, Tennessee. Davy and Elizabeth eventually had four children of their own. Davy bought land along the creek and built a **mill** to grind grain, a factory to make gunpowder, and a **distillery.** All three businesses made money. In 1817, the Tennessee **legislature** made Davy **justice of the peace** for the area of Shoal Creek. When people of the area had arguments, Davy decided who was right and who was wrong.

Helping Tennessee

Wherever Davy Crockett went, he told stories about his adventures that made people smile and laugh. Crockett's stories made him popular with other people who lived in the state of Tennessee. Davy decided to use his stories, and the **fame** that came with them, to help the **citizens** of Tennessee. He traveled around the state, asking people to elect him to the **legislature.** Crockett was elected in 1821 and again in 1823.

Crockett **campaigned** for a seat in the Tennessee legislature. Many people listened to his stories and ideas about the government.

Davy Crockett was a member of the Tennessee legislature in 1821–1822 and again in 1823–1824.

In 1821, Shoal Creek flooded and washed away Crockett's businesses. All the Crocketts' money had been used to build the businesses. Crockett had to start all over again, but he decided to do it somewhere else. The Crockett family moved again, this time to the northwestern end of Tennessee, near the Obion River.

Congress

While he was in the **legislature,** Davy worked to help poor people own land. Davy thought he could do more if he went to work in the **Congress** in Washington, D.C. The voters of Tennessee elected him to Congress in 1827 and 1829. Davy tried to pass a law that would let poor people use **vacant** land. However, the law was not passed while he was in Congress.

Like Father, Like Son

Crockett's son, John Wesley, was elected to Congress after Crockett died. He was able to pass the Vacant Land Law a few years after the Battle of the Alamo.

As a member of government, Davy still **entertained** people with his stories.

U.S. president Andrew Jackson served from 1829 to 1837.

Congressman Crockett also made President Andrew Jackson angry. Jackson wanted Congress to pass a law called the Indian Removal Act. The law would take away the land of Native American tribes living east of the Mississippi River and give the land to white families. Davy thought this was unfair and voted against it. This disagreement lost the election for Davy in 1831. Davy was elected again in 1833, but lost the election in 1835 because he disagreed with President Jackson over bank laws.

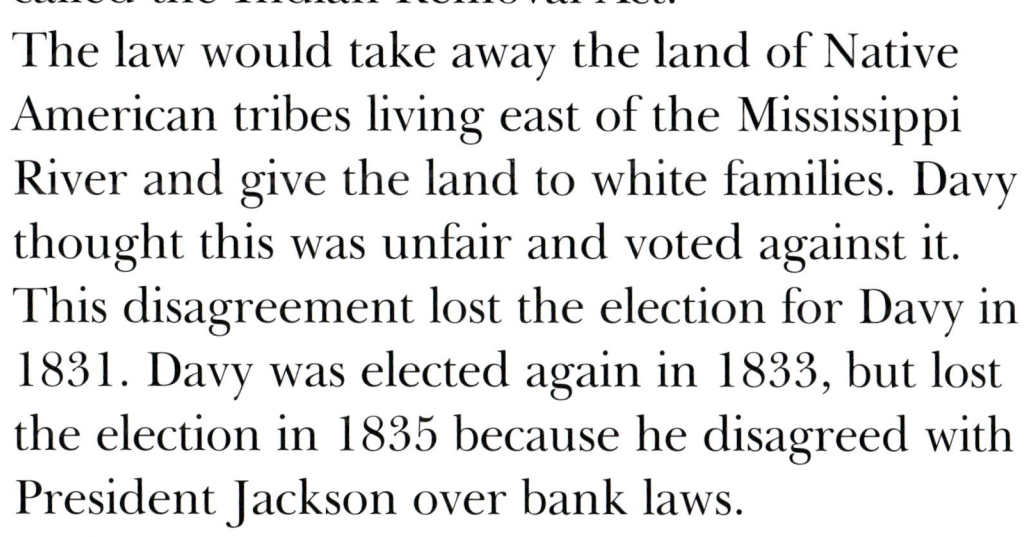

Words to Live By

Davy's motto in life was, "Be always sure you are right, then go ahead."

Disappointment

When Crockett lost the election in 1835, he was very disappointed. He was angry with the rich leaders of **Congress** for not giving poor people in the United States a chance to have their own land. Crockett was tired of following rules. He wanted to go to a place where he could start his life all over again. He chose Texas. At that time, Texas still belonged to the country of Mexico.

The United States, 1837

This map shows how the land of the United States was divided in 1837.

Although he was no longer a young man, Crockett still enjoyed the adventures of the frontier.

Crockett packed up his belongings and said good-bye to his family. He would never see them again. As he traveled from Tennessee to Texas, Crockett had many adventures. He entered in shooting contests, hunted buffalo, and even wrestled a cougar!

25

Remember the Alamo!

When Crockett arrived in Texas, he went to the Alamo in San Antonio. Crockett had been promised land if he would fight for Texas. For thirteen days, Crockett and the other Texans were able to hold off the Mexican army. But on the thirteenth day, General Santa Anna's men attacked the **fort** one last time. They were able to get over the walls with ladders. Davy and his men did not have time to reload their guns, so they swung their rifles like baseball bats at the Mexican soldiers.

Davy (right) and the Texan defenders did the best they could when fighting the Mexican soldiers.

The actual Battle of San Jacinto lasted less than 20 minutes. Only 9 of the 910 Texas soldiers were killed, and 30 were injured.

Santa Anna did not want anyone left alive in the fort. At the end of the fighting, Davy and a few other Texans **surrendered.** Santa Anna ordered his officers to kill Davy with their swords.

Six weeks later, General Sam Houston and the Texans fought Santa Anna's army at the San Jacinto River. The Texans yelled, "Remember the Alamo!" in honor of those who had died. Texas won the battle and the war when Santa Anna was captured.

The 28th State

Texas joined the United States in 1845. Texas is the only state in the United States that used to be a separate country.

Remembering Davy

Davy Crockett was able to make many people happy by telling his stories. In a time before televisions, movies, and libraries in almost every town, Crockett gave people a chance to be **entertained.**

A young boy reads about Davy Crockett in 1955 while wearing a coon skin cap and a Davy Crockett t-shirt.

In Honor of a Hero
The town of Crockett, Texas, was named for Davy in 1837—one year after he died.

Crockett tried to help people who could not help themselves. He protected the other school children from a bully when he was a boy. He helped poor people in the United States by trying to pass laws to give them land. He fought to make Texas free. Some men are remembered for the words they wrote, or the things they built. Davy Crockett is remembered for fighting for freedom.

> Davy Crockett was always ready to fight for what he believed in.

Glossary

campaign try to get people to vote for you
citizen person who lives in a city, town, state, or country
commander person in charge of an army
Congress part of U.S. government that makes the laws
debt money owed to somebody
distillery building in which liquor is made
entertain provide amusement
fame being well-known and well thought of by people
fort strong building used for defense against enemy attack
frontiersman person who explores unsettled areas, particularly in the United States
harbor part of a body of water where ships dock
justice of the peace person responsible for making sure laws are followed
legislature group of people who make laws
militia group of soldiers called to fight in an emergency
mill building in which grain is made into flour
surrender give oneself to someone else of higher power
tavern place where people go for food and drinks
vacant not used

More Books to Read

Adler, David A. *A Picture Book of Davy Crockett*. New York: Holiday House, 1998.

Alphin, Elaine Marie. *Davy Crockett*. Minneapolis, Minn.: Lerner Publications Company, 2003.

Feeney, Kathy. *Davy Crockett*. Minnetonka, Minn.: Bridgestone Books, 2002.

Harmon, Daniel E. *Davy Crockett*. Broomall, Penn.: Chelsea House Publishing, 2001.

Marvis, B. *Davy Crockett*. Broomall, Penn.: Chelsea House Publishing, 2003.

Sullivan, George. *Davy Crockett*. New York: Scholastic Reference, 2001.

Places to Visit

Davy Crockett Birthplace State Park
1245 Davy Crockett Park Road
Limestone, TN 37681-5825
Visitor Information: (423) 257-2167

Acton State Park
5800 Park Rd 21
Cleburne, TX 76031
Visitor Information: (817) 645-4215

Index

Alamo 4–5, 7, 22, 26–27

Baltimore, Maryland 12

Congress 22–23, 24
Creek 17
Creek War 7, 18
Crockett, John 6, 7, 14, 15
Crockett, John Wesley 16, 22
Crockett, Margaret 17
Crockett, Rebecca 6
Crockett, William 16

Finley, Mary (Polly) 6, 14–15, 16, 17, 18

Jackson, Andrew 23

Kennedy, John 14–15

legislature 7, 19, 20, 22

Mexico 4, 5, 24
militia 17
mills 7, 19

Patton, Elizabeth 18

Santa Anna, Antonio López de 5, 26, 27
school 10–11
Shoal Creek 19, 21

taverns 7, 9, 13
Tennessee 6, 7, 9, 13, 16, 17, 19, 20–21, 22, 25
Texas 4, 5, 24, 25, 26, 27, 28, 29
Travis, William 5

Washington, D.C. 22
Wilson, Abraham 14

Virginia 9, 11, 12